pilgrims, immigrants, and refugees

Luke H. Snyder

Pilgrims, Immigrants, and Refugees
by Luke H. Snyder
Copyright © 2025 by Luke H. Snyder

All rights reserved.
No part of this book may be reproduced, stored in a retrieval system, or transmitted in any form or by any means—electronic, mechanical, photocopying, recording, or otherwise—without the prior written permission of the author, except for brief quotations used in reviews or scholarly works, as permitted by copyright law.

For permissions or inquiries, please contact:
Luke H. Snyder
Email: lukehenrysnyder@gmail.com

This is a work of poetry. Any resemblance to actual persons, places, or events is purely coincidental.

Published by Banana Moon Farms
Printed in the United States of America
First Edition, July 2025

ISBN 979-8-9991150-1-0

This book was self-published through Amazon Kindle Direct Publishing (KDP).

For Susan Ruth Ivy Snyder

"Mother"

Go Rebels!

/*forward*

when i wrote *Heartstrings and Harmonies,* i was trying to make
sense of the past —
the love, the loss,
the pins and needles in my chest.
laying everything out,
unfiltered
naked.

this book is different.
Pilgrims, Immigrants, and Refugees is not
just about where i've been —
it's about where we're all going.
searching
leaving behind
rebuilding
understanding

these poems were born on the road between what was and
what might be. they help carry the movements—
internal, mental, emotional, generational.
what it means to belong and what it costs to keep
pretending we aren't lost.

if you've started or are starting over—
longing for home in a place you just arrived—
or find yourself trying to make meaning out this jigsaw
puzzle we call *life* —

then let's take a walk, again.

Luke H. Snyder

/pilgrims, immigrants, and refugees

the battle-worn
have risen
into the sky
to fight again

because even peace
would not follow
a soul whose eyes
have seen too much

they left behind
scars
medals
and love letters
so burned they could only be written
in ash

even heaven has a battlefield
and they
were called to duty

/ henry ivy

a heron
cuts through the night
the same way
i cut through memory

the moon
knows where it's going
i pretend
i do too

i am chasing quilts again
stitched by hands
that don't reach for me anymore

the sawgrass
leans towards something holy
and i follow
because i have nothing
left to lose

/flight

like a hair tie
i was made to hold things together
but no one warned me
how often that means
losing myself

i cling to loose threads
of people
of memories
of almosts

i stretch
i twist
i tangle

until what once held shape
is now a knot
too tight
to undo

/ *hair ties*

it's hard to have peace
when no one has the patience
to listen

everyone's talking
but no one hears

we can't fix the world
if we don't slow down
long enough
to understand each other

/ everyone is misunderstood

a wise friend once said
"…a pair of eyes to see the lies, so why does it hold the puppets…"

we keep dancing
on strings

one day
we will tangle
and call it madness

/good intentions

when did
pieces of me by ashlee simpson
stop being a song
and start becoming
my autobiography

/on a monday, i am waiting

sticks and stones
and the pieces you left behind

i gathered them all
with trembling hands
to build a bridge

/=^=^=^=^=^=^=\

only to
burn
alone

/ sticks and stones

you don't understand me
because i am debt
buried deep in borrowed bones
surviving on the borrowed air of another day

time hangs above my head
if i could
i would erase it all
but instead i wait —
for the seventh year to come
when the circle folds back
and i become the same story again

/ insufficiant funds

no names
no strings
no goodbye

just stars
burning holes
in the sky

i don't know
if it was real
but i remember
how it
set fire
to my chest

/ strangers

can you smell
the roses
wilting at my feet
as i scrub
the blood and memory
from my skin
with water
they told me
was holy

i wanted it to save me
instead
it stung

can you hear
the angels
or is that just
the sound of me
trying to breathe
as i walk away
from everything
that once
felt like god

/ *holy water*

you keep running
searching for peace
as if distance
can mend what's broken

when the cracks appear
you walk away
as if leaving
could make them disappear

one foot dances
too scared to fall
the other reaches
to forget it all

you try to breathe
but the past
clings to your sleeve
like it belongs there

you drift
but never move
a ghost in the window
trapped in the glass

you run from lies
that never died
they live behind your eyes
waiting

you try to breathe
but the past
clings to your sleeve
like it owns you

and still you search

but everything
feels the same
as if the fire
was born with your name

no matter the miles
no matter the years
the past
will find you
and pull you back in

you try to breathe
but the past
clings to your sleeve

/ the past won't let go

you came like a wildflower
after the fire
lifted me from ashes

but like smoke
you vanished
and i
kept burning

you don't call
i wait
alone
for a voice
that once knew mine

i trace your name
into dust on the window
and watch it
disappear with the sun

i hope you never feel
what tugs at my chest

like dandelions
blown
too far to come back

but still
i wait
hoping
you'll call
just
once
more

/in the dust of the windowpane

we are still asleep

on golden nails —

as the dust

clings to our tongues

bitter and old

yet —

we keep walking

into fire

and calling it

freedom

/*untitled*

we said
we would be there
for each other
through rain or shine
but all we do
is drown
in the sea we built

/ levels

my dreams
do not belong
in your world

i push you away
because i am still becoming

this is the last stop
on a runaway train
to nowhere

when i arrive
you will understand

the road i walked
is made from
the shattered pieces
of myself

/ dreams shape one's journey

do you mind
if i sit beside you
just for a while
my head is tired
my heart is heavier

if i wronged you
under your father's eyes
will you still
share your bread

◻

there is blood
on the table
but no one moves
no one speaks
is this our last supper

◻

tell me the story of
those dark days
was it hell
or a holy riddle
three long nights of silence

◻

there is food
on the table
and blood
in our mouths
is this the last gathering of

◻

the wind shifts the cloth
have we already
read the ending
and still
said nothing

◻

knocking comes from within
like ghosts
we pretend not to believe

does it matter
now

◻

tell me again
your story

was it hell
was it grace

or just
another cave
you
escaped

/ the last great carpenter

god
is a little boy
with too much imagination

his hands
still learning
how to hold the world

forgive him
he is trying

/jesus was an alien

i have an infected pedicle
my soul
wears out
as the the night
continues
but only my eyes
know how to glow

my mind
like a hallway
reaching for doors
escaping?
spiraling?
chasing beating hearts
beneath these floorboards

only the curve
of my rising horns
remembers the light
through the door frame

/ *the shining*

hey god
or whoever's up there

can you hear me
because i'm tired

just want a little peace
in my head
and to feel okay
in my skin

/in need of a miracle

standing between
what once was
and still remains

i run my hand
along the rough bark
of a redwood
and centuries
press into my skin

they have seen fire
storms
clearcut grief
and still
they rise
reaching past the fog
into something holy

these forests
have outlived everything
we thought was permanent
holding the disappearances
in its rings

every fallen branch
every root
here
in the ancient
and alive
i realize
how small i am
how little
my problems matter
to something
that's been breathing
for a thousand years

they don't need us
they never did
we're the visitors
just passing through

and maybe
that's the point

/*giants used to hold the sky up*

we've dreamt of freedom
a life without chains
but here we are
still dancing in the dark
as hope slips
through our fingers
like sand
and yet
everyday we reach
for the light switch
to try to move on

/ same old song and dance

a soul that's been stricken
starts to soften
just from one kiss

and suddenly
all those scars?
aren't hidden anymore

what's left
is this raw hunger
for something simple —
warmth, closeness, real

/ *hards scars*

the world
so quick to judge
so eager to call it a *plague*
never knowing what it means
to carry another
to walk in the shoes
of those who are
crushed—
forgotten—
erased—

they mock the change
the turn of fate
blind to the truth
unaware that karma wears
its own face—
its own name—
waiting to teach the lesson:

we are all vulnerable to change

how easy it is to condemn
what we do not understand
until the tables turn
until the *"plague"* creeps
to those who once pointed fingers
and they, too, must seek help
from the very hands they once pushed away

i've seen it with my own eyes —
"these" people
living in a world that hate them
fighting daily for something
as simple as acceptance
for the right to love,
to be loved

in their final years
they still stand tall
still carry more grace
than anyone should have to
they give
even when their own lives are running out
putting others first
fighting not just to survive
but to be seen as human
in a world that forgets
what it means to be human

i praise them
those who endure
who fight for their lives,
for their love,
in a world that would rather erase *"them"*
than understand them

they are the strong ones
not the ones who judge
but the ones who rise
again and again
after every fall

/ angels in america

aren't we all
seeking asylum
from something

building ships
out of whatever
floats

aren't we all just
pilgrims
immigrants
and
refugees

/ white flags

future days
will taste like sun
on my skin

salt in my hair
mountains watching me breathe
firewood stacked
earth steady beneath my bare feet

i want freedom
not outside
but in the quiet
corners of my mind

where i dance
between who i was
and who
i am becoming

two selves
pulling at the same thread
each begging
to be seen

the monsters
sit beside me at night
gentle and familiar

the demons
know my name

but the humans —
they smile
holding knives behind their backs

/*unmasking*

i feel it
your face reflected in the waters
of the lion's den

forsaken
i will stand at your feet
on the iron throne

the power that says
this is destined to be
more than a story
more than fiction

/ *something greater*

father — strike your lightning
ignite the fire
let your thunder shake this town
until there's nothing left to take
but me and my thoughts
and the sound of my scream

i am who i am
but i cannot carry this any longer

father — send your wisdom
send a prayer
bring your healing hands
until i feel the spark
of my revival
the rise of my power
and the roar of my soul

i am who i am
but i cannot bear this any longer

/<><

i'm awake
but the night
refuses to let me go

send me
another angel
maybe this one
will learn to stay

/ restless leg syndrome

lost and alone
tossed by the tide
no place to call home

carried by currents
forever searching
never found

/ driftwood

would you
drown in your tears
let them carry you away

or gather the pieces
to dry your eyes
and stand beneath
the wild sky

would you meet
the fear inside
let shadows see the light

would you turn
run from the dark
hoping it turns
into grey

would you fight
or drift
lost
in a stormy sea

/perfect storm

a splitting heart
a mind that won't take a second to breathe
days trying to catch up with
the dust caught in the wind

i am
searching
for a way
to start again

/fly back home

what is home
is it the place i once lived
or the memories
that won't let me sleep

is it where i felt whole
or where i forgot
how to feel safe

is it a dream
i made up
or one
i'm still waiting for

/four walls and a roof

walking down the street lost in thought
the world spins
and i spin against
the noise
the chaos
the fear
the confusion
and i can't seem to find my way out

sometimes it feels like i'm alone
but i know i'm not
there's a light within me
that grows brighter
when i stop looking

i will find my place
in this wild world

/ finding my pearl

when i was a kid
we had a science teacher
who taught from a magic bus
all i remember her say was
yellowstone could blow any day now
that it would block the sun
freeze the earth
wipe us out

and somehow
that stuck harder
than anything else i learned

she turned my imagination
into a doomsday clock

funny
how fear
is better at teaching
than most textbooks

maybe that's why
i still flinch
when the sky looks off

and why
i never really trusted
a sunny day again

i wish i had remembered
something more
than just
the end of the world

/ our science teacher loved rubber ducks

funny
how easy it is
to trap animals

just give them a taste
of what they're starving for

even the wild
will kneel
if the liar
feeds them first

/false prophets

we are all born
into a house
gifted by a power
too vast to understand

we carry our purpose
through storms not of our making
under free will —
open a door
close a door
break a window
pop a tire on the fast lane
eat fast food every night
recycle the compost
fight for justice
fight for peace
fight the war
heal the victims
heal ourselves
embrace another
stop at stop signs
run red lights

but we cannot
flip our hourglass

/ *riders on the storm*

hot metal
cuts across blue skies
heads stay still
legs carry us forward
arms raised to battle
but why
do we keep fighting
when our hearts want peace

/*war is the answer*

running on fumes
buzzed off smoke
life's slipping
but i'm still here

always rushing
just to sit still

the dogs bailed
on the meat wagon
as sunday floats by
like it forgot something

ticks drop
off the deer's back
and i ease into the saddle
like it's where i was headed
all along

/ *running on empty*

there is
a parasite
in my mind

i feel it

with every breath
i take

/ there's a tick inside my brain

what does the caterpillar think
as it sheds its skin
revealing the chrysalis —
clinging to the world like velcro

does it remember the pain
of digesting itself
or does it forget
as its mind rattles with transformation

when it emerges
a butterfly —
does it just fly away
seeking food
leaving behind its past
without a second glance

and is that what becomes of us
trapped in cycles
driven by hunger and shelter
working so hard to escape
that we forget to savor the life we've been given

are we the caterpillar
or the butterfly
or both —
desperate to break free
searching for an afterlife
forgetting that we are already here
not yet a butterfly
not yet free
but alive in the here and now

/*cocoon*

the glass sponge
oldest living soul
anchored to the ocean floor
a delicate skeleton
of glass and silence

it filters the world —
plankton, bacteria,
passing through
its still body
as if it has all the time
in the world

11,000 years
of enduring beauty
but does it know
does it think
does it dream of other currents

it doesn't move
but leaves pieces
of itself behind
in the water
an ancient trail
of persistence

/ the glass sponge

if i'm not worth keeping
then don't lock me
in the icebox

/gone fishin'

just floating
through time —

days pass
but none of it
really sticks

what are we even chasing?

/ the fox

what's all this noise about
are we stuck in the same loop
just going round and round
waiting to find some peace

why all these distractions anyway
are we just running
from the quiet moments
too scared to sit with ourselves
and all the emptiness we carry

maybe we're just searching
to feel whole again
trying to fix the cracks
hoping someday
we'll cruise down the smooth road

/ re(grinds)

my eyes may have been blind
but my heart stayed anchored
i need the truth
before i leave
are you mine
or am i just a fool to stay

/gesture for the jester

the dirt
on your knees
and on your nose
is the same

only you
know if it's yours
or theirs

———————

you make promises
the way others breathe

under the sun
you bury
every truth

because fun
matters more
than honesty

/gypsy woman

there must
be some kind of reason
why i watched you
slip away
so quietly
into sedation

someone keeps
knocking
at the window
is it the devil
or cupid
with bad aim

is this love
or is it
the high
i can't tell
if you're hiding
or if i'm refusing
to see

who am i
in your life
you've already used
every excuse
and i am
out of reasons

i saw your ghost
dancing in the driveway
as you speak
in smoke
and soft promises
but silence
hurts more than any lie

is this love
or just
what's left of it

i don't know
when i stopped
pulling you back
maybe
i just got tired
of standing in the fire
while you
learned how to disappear

/ used up all your temptations

i met maggie
when we were too young to understand
why the sky turned grey

after years apart
she howled
at the moon
with balloons
in her hands
and a void
in her heart

but wild girls
burn
and fall fast

little maggie
on the horizon
brush your hair
from your eyes
you're not a fool tonight

/ always stay clean, maggie

you want to keep running
but i want to stay and take a break

we drag each other down
what a shame
what a soft
slow
shame

/ stop draggin' my heart around

your message
loud and clear

(sent)

…:….:….:…*error 404*

the recipient address
no longer exists

/ lost connection

the river rushes high
crashing through my veins
the devil pierced my arms
now blood stains my skin
when will this end
i don't really know
so i sit back
and let the chaos unfold

/ *rivers and veins*

a half-healed runaway patient
on the edge of forgetting myself

but i still
hold the whiskey
like it's my last prayer

a memory you stepped over
just a genie with no wishes
left to grant

still
the poison
never touches my lips

/ this shit is redundant

leaving home
losing a piece of myself
my insides unravel
the bus skips stops
but my body wants to pause
to spill what it cannot hold

the driver waits
but the road moves forward
and i am not sure if i will

a new life
faster than fear can catch
what did i say yes to?
what have i done?
wipe the tears
stand taller

south to georgia
north to tennessee
the mountains
calling me onward

they teach the dogs to hunt
turn boys into men
girls into women
and remind us
never to look back

/*southbound — northbound*

my fragile bones and broken skull
drift away
like a ship without anchor
pulled by the moon's tide
and kissed by the sun's light
lost
out at sea

/jolly roger

sink or swim
the tides are rising
time to cut the anchor free

black flag
waves upon the stag
let them all see

/ uncharted territory

a runaway train
no brakes
just me
racing through despair

your judgment?
already left the station
lost somewhere in the night

and me?
i don't mind
watching my hours slip away —
until i realize
sometimes the tracks
lead right back home

/ soul asylum

i fell so deep
i forgot what i was chasing
solace or the high — hard to tell

faith didn't come with me
just the shadows
and my own tears,
like rain stuck on repeat

but maybe
the light isn't outside
maybe it's been waiting
in the cracks i tried to hide from all along

/first night alone in a hotel room

up here on my high horse
the cold is creeping in
i'm losing my grip
on all these feelings inside

/ black and white sunset

i lied
when i told you i was fine
lost in my mind
again

i lied
when i said everything was alright
losing myself
again

sometimes
i drift in my own space
some things never
change

sometimes
my mistakes
hurt too much
to change

/ *i'm fine*

forgive me mama
for i have sinned

in my mistakes
i lost my way

but in your love
i find my home again

/ teach me to heal

not sure
what's worse —
my brain won't shut up
or my body won't stop hurting

some days
it all just blends together

/*one man show*

i am nothing
if i am something
trapped
in this body
that feels more like a cage

every thought
is a question
every step
a confession

i am something
if not nothing
we are drowning
in this life
pretending to breathe

built a home
on soft gravel
and still
called it safe

i see it
in the mirror
the cracks
around my eyes

but i will not
lie down
and wait for mercy

i will break when they lay me down
not before
everything behind me
is falling apart

yet
i am still
standing

i am breathing
but i am tired
and if i lose
everything
tomorrow

at least
i will know
i did not
pretend
to smile

i see it
in the mirror
the cracks
around my eyes

no
i will not
roll over

i will not
wait

i will stand
until i can't
and even then
i'll try

/ still somehow

i thought
i'd tasted every bad apple life threw at me

quietly
i waited
for a wake-up call

but maybe
i'm still chewing
and the soul i'm chasing
is just the next bite

/ before the apple fell

the leaves can't decide what to be
and neither can i
the days get darker
but the years?
they're just speeding by like they don't care

/ dale earnhardt

chemicals
just floating around —
like secrets you didn't ask for
but can't stop noticing

breath by breath,
the mystery's in the air
whether you like it or not

/ *chem trails*

i crawl in
through your eyes
a mess — broken

you hear me
splitting your ears
my cries hanging there

shake me loose
take in this lost refugee
give me something real
to hold on to

/*rescue me*

hold me
until you awaken
until my thoughts race
spinning in circles around you

hold me
until you see my smile
until the cracks in my skin
fall away, piece by piece

hold me
until you sleep
until your eyes, heavy
in love with me

hold me
until your last breath
until your body fades
and your spirit hovers

/ *in your arms*

we dance
on twigs and pebbles
with grace
and broken feet
still —
we move

/ air guitar

see me
in the house
that built my bones

in the windows
i still look through

too tender
to let go
of the things
that became me

/ *let things go*

there's an old house in the country
silent, cracked — barely standing
sunlight sneaks through broken windows
wildflowers clutch the walls like they're holding on

it's been abandoned for years
but it's not empty
memories live here —
some soft, some sharp enough to bleed

it doesn't just hold stories —
it's waiting
for someone to add the next chapter
someone who's lost enough to listen

/forgotten in the will

follow the wild horse
to where the earth's drinking

rest your head
in some cool shade

take in the tall grass smell
let the birds sing you their songs

/ *hell of a way to go*

here is the river,
                breaking into scattered white

a swallow slices the sky,
                too quick for my eyes to follow

the dam holds back what once flowed free

my heart breaks with every fish it forgets,
                everything upstream is dying
quietly

stuck between the rage and the still

a broken promise,
                the dam says it's helping

/sestet #6

i fear the day
i have it all figured out

better to live
in the dance of the unknown

/ untitled (2)

born in the usa
just a little too late

i wish i heard johnny's chords
or watched the king
move like thunder in his hips

some days
i really do
wish time
worked backwards

/ tupelo and kingsland

i once saw a quote written with construction paper
in an elementary school classroom

"music is life, that's why our hearts beat"

but what happens
when it skips a beat

is it just a pause

~

or a sign something's wrong
when the symphony resumes
do we pick up where we left off
or do we race to catch up

when heartache strikes
do we play the wrong chord
are we no longer in tune
our rhythms lost
our bodies heating
over 98 degrees
sweating
as the next note hangs heavy
a verse we're not ready for

do we skip it
walk to the beat of another drum
{1&2&3&4&}
until our hearts find their rhythm
vibrating in harmony with life's song

/ middle C

you gain nothing
without the courage
to stretch your hand
failure is no shame
when you have chosen
to try anyway
and that choice
is the bravest
love you can give yourself

/ success is in the trying

who keeps paying
for this shit
these magazines stacked at checkout
next to gum and batteries
like they belong there
like they're essential

glossy covers
quietly selling insecurities
"ten ways to fix yourself"
"the truth about happiness"
as if they know themselves

they tell us what to wear
what to fear
what to chase
what to hate
and we follow
scrolling
flipping
liking
buying

as if the next page
might finally mean something

but it never does
just more glitter on garbage

/propaganda poets society

the a/c's just blowing hot air
sticking to everything
while ash floats
from an unfiltered camel
finding every crack in this rusted ford

john anderson's voice
scratching through the speakers
like he's been here too long

i guess i'm helping gramps
trim his rose bushes again
while the world
keeps growing wild around us

/ king farm

i look up at the american flag
and wonder if Betsy Ross knew what she was making at the time
i think of everyone
who crossed oceans
borders
and language
to stand beneath it

a stitched-up story of what we stood for
what we lost —
what we still pretend to be

other countries wave theirs
like warnings
an X marks the place
some stacked in stripes and boxes
like they're fighting themselves

but look at ours

thirteen stripes

red for the fight —
blood and sacrifice

white for the faith —
love and peace

like open wounds and bandages
like freedom isn't free

a field of blue
trying to hold it all together
fifty stars
still hoping

they mean the same thing

this flag isn't perfect
but neither are we
and still —
we're here

/ star spangled banner

sitting in the driveway
engine still running
rain drowning the windshield

my son asleep
in the back seat
breath soft
like a bedside prayer

this is the moment
my heart has been bleeding for
this peace —
making it through another storm together

/40 days and 40 nights

swallow me whole
connecticut

pull me under
tennessee

drag me between
your muddy shores
and spit me out
somewhere
downriver

let the current
cleanse
everything
i used to be

and when i'm
bare
as chantilly lace
baptize me
mississippi

show me
what it means
to begin again

/ bathe in the river

the old concrete business
laid out like bones
on the front lawn
form boards pretending to be garden art
tractors and excavators
frozen in time
since 1988
with one name
still painted on the doors

i stare at the rust
and wonder
if i could spark it all back to life
reshape it into something
that matters now

how did it all slip
from building foundations
to becoming one
buried beneath them

/cloud 35

the axe handles
stretch like spines
into the mountains

men went marching
on broken prayers

the wind
was the only thing
that returned
carrying stories —
"go john henry!"

they were promised
white sand
for gold dust
but found
blisters —
chains —
and graves
marked and taxed
<u>progress</u>

how many hands
had to splinter
before they learned
that american dream
was just
another war
in disguise

/ bones in the mountains

appalachians to the whites
they walked the ridgelines
barefoot and hungry
before your signs
grew teeth

"trespassers will be shot on sight" —

you forget
they were there
long before
you learned
how to aim

/ don't tread on me

you've waited in the weeds
for the wind to move
but the world
has been slow to shift

    if the sky fell tomorrow
    would you still wait your turn

you dream of dusty roads
and broken lanterns
hoping the path
will wash you clean

    you count your scars
    like stories
    looking for a silver line

they call you a quitter
from the safety of their couch
but they've never held
the cards you were dealt

    no one claps at show and tell
    when you bring water
    from the deepest well
    it's only holy
    when a man in a hat
    says so

/ here comes the silence before the thunder

the moon pulls at me
like i'm made of ocean
but it's not love
it's gravity

i thought it was you
calling me home
but maybe
it's just the pain
of being lonely
at high tide

/*waves crashing on the shore*

every message
i threw into the ocean
keeps washing up
at my feet

salt-soaked
burning wounds
i thought would heal

no matter how far
i try to send it
the tide
knows my handwriting

/*message in a bottle*

waking up
to sunlight —

somewhere else
someone —

last breath

/ *we are the lucky ones*

there's always
a new low
just when you think
you've found
the bottom
life hands you
a shovel
and says —
dig

rock bottom
has a basement

maybe plant something
while you're down there
help come up through the cracks

/guest room below

just a mirror
falling apart —
too busy loving
its own reflection
to notice the cracks
beneath the surface

spiraling out
dizzy
from looking
too long
at itself

/ *narcissist*

come back to me —

someone who knows
what it means to be broken

and still wants to stay
just to be free
with me —

not because i'm waiting
because i'm ready

/ *refugee*

why do i keep seeing you
bright red —
in empty buildings
like you're the only
life left there —
a spirit stronghold
hanging on
in all that mess

where is the one
who holds your heart?

are you
rebuilding yourself
in the ruins too?

/cardinal

shakedown street
ain't the same anymore
the colors faded
like a tie-dye shirt left in the sun

what once smelled like incense and revolution
now reeks of nostalgia
sold out for quieter music

it was never just a street
it was a feeling
and feelings
don't live here anymore

/gratefully dead

i was too busy
soaring through storms
chasing the sun

to notice

someone
clipped my wings
miles ago

no wonder
the fall
felt like my fault

/ a couple miles back

i reached the county line
only to be thrown back
by the same wind
i thought would carry me

that country mile
twisted around me
like a tornado
in no rush
to let me go

/*county line*

when i get nervous
i reach for something sweet
but the cabinets are empty
so i chew on adderall
like it's candy
like it knows something
i don't

i watch the world
turn another degree
as i pace by the window
like it's a finish line

some guy downtown sells maps
says the path is short
the fee is modest
but every road he points to
ends in therapy—like healing
was the wrong destination

sing me a hymn from the basement
where the light never reaches the mice

i was baptized in a coffee can
and raised in the ashes
of a marlboro light
i was born from a kiss on the go
raised by the hiss of a radio
that only played half the truth

i lived off
truths wrapped in dares
thinking they were signs
clipped coupons
like they were lifelines

if love
was on the bottom shelf
i bought two

the clouds came carrying unpaid debts
this town forgot how to lie
but still remembers
how to bury
what it can't fix

i raise a glass
to the ghosts
who never took shit
and still rattle
when the thunder rolls by

so sing it again
that basement hymn
the one soaked
in dust and static

i came from smoke and engine noise
from people who ran
before they ever arrived

and still
i haven't stopped
moving

/ *hiss of the radio*

it's been raining
for thirteen weekends straight

you start to wonder
if someone's pulling the strings
keeping us inside
until we run out of fresh air to breathe

or maybe
it's just mother nature
weeping
another omen
for what we've done to her

and we
deserve
every drop

/13

i'd pack a bag and disappear
thinking the world
was ready with all the answers

but it wouldn't
take a whole trip
around the sun
to admit —
i have no clue what i'm doing

maybe running was
never the problem
maybe i just thought somewhere else
meant something clearer

/ around the world in 80 days

does a leaf think about the perfect time to fall,
                              a soft spiral, a sudden drop —

or is it just tired of holding on
to something that no longer feeds it

does it trust the wind to carry it somewhere softly

we gather them up like they're guilty,
                              like they're trash —

spreading poison—dumping chemicals,
                                  better than thy neighbor —

then we wonder why the lawn looks dead in spring

/ sestet #7

some days
i wish there was a pause
where —
i had no address
no past i keep rewriting
no future waiting

just the freedom
to disappear
without a reason
or a warning

three days
wandering like a ghost
in a country that never knew my name

sleeping where the sky says yes
eating when my body remembers how
getting high
just to feel the water from the stars
instead of expectations —

sometimes
the unrooting calls
looking for soil that doesn't
spit back out

/*vagabond*

the wind doesn't blow
through the needles
unless it needs to

the pines don't lean for fun
they're showing you something
old as bone —

sometimes the devil
wears your own face
and the hardest battle
is the one inside

he's never on your side —
but sometimes
you forget that too

/ earth angel

fog slips in
around the back of the mountain
softly —
like an elk breath

hard to say
if this is heaven
or smoke rising
from something burning
far below

either way —
same stone
same sky

/ *monadnock*

buttercups and dandelions
take over the lawn —
yellow scatter in spring wind
not part of the plan

it's not perfect
neither are we

but this is how life comes back —
rooted deep in soil
almost as if it were
spread with our hands

no reason to mow it down
just because it's not suburban green

let them drive by
we know what it took
to make this ground
breathe

/buttercups and dandelions

first
they take the penny —
copper gone to melt
more bullets than butterfly wings

then the nickel
thick as a blade
slips through the pockets

the dime rolls away
like water on stone

the quarter —
vanishes
from the clatter of parking meters
swipe your plastic for a bag high fructose corn syrup

until
only paper remains —
creased, marked, owned
by dirty hands you'll never shake

coming and going
like wind
through a fence of bones

/ *down the current goes the currency*

everybody wants
wildflowers
scattered color-bursts
to gather in mason jars
on the kitchen windowsills

but i was raised
walking barefoot
in summers
where the red clover grows

my grandfather
never spoke of beauty
only soil
and how clover
keeps it from washing away

his hands —
calloused like bark
taught me
what stays
and what simply looks good

wildflowers
come and go
a flash of color
in a life full of leaving

but the clover
holds the hill
holds the story
of the ones who stayed

/ everybody wants wildflowers

stardust—
what we are
what we eat

a look
a hand on the back
a bowl passed across the table

we feed each other
without thinking
ash and atoms
split and shared

even silence
is something chewed

/ *ziggy stardust*

i ate myself
because no one else would feed me

bit by bit
until all that was left
was a napkin
with my name on it

i was starving
for love
for peace
for someone to stop me

but hunger
makes monsters
out of mirrors

/ *self-eating sandwich*

heavy
is the handle
of the broom
when it's your mess
you're sweeping up

every motion
a memory
every dust pile
a regret

no one claps
for cleaning the disaster
you created
but still
you sweep
because someone's gotta
and this time
it's you

/ *dust bunnies*

everyone is standing in line
waiting for the next mayflower
as if it's a real ship
with wooden planks and white sails
as if salvation is coming
docked at some harbor

but the mayflower
was never just a ship
it was a movement
and movements
don't wait for permission
they begin
when someone decides
to set sail
on their own

/*pilgrims were everyday people*

it's quiet out here
moonlight on tombstones
names I don't know
some chipped off
some half-eaten
by wind and rain
forgotten—

who spoke them last?
what hands worked?
what trails walked?

not much left
but this
and the night
slipping between
pine roots

/ *old stones*

the crow is back
been tracking me
a black fleck in grey skies—
comes down with eyes
older than my name

lost like a refugee
wandering this skin
an immigrant
from the breath between worlds

a gopher pokes up
in the early haze
sees his shadow
dirt still wet
rain still coming
rain still coming
rain still coming
rain still coming

might need the boat again
point the nose
to another
south

/ that damn crow again

the headless horseman has returned
but this time
he rides from within
no blade
no battle cry
just a low bellow
we don't need ghosts
to haunt us anymore
we are doing that just fine on our own

the end times —

end the genocide
end the war
end the poverty

before it becomes
another chapter
in a book
we pretend
to teach

history
is not repeating itself
we are

/ *sleepy and hollow*

/ the end

Thank you for going for a walk with, *Pilgrims, Immigrants, and Refugees*.
Every poem in these pages was written with a questioning heart—and I hope you never stop asking why, trying to make sense of it all.
If this book moved you, please consider leaving a review on Amazon.
Your words help independent authors like me reach new readers.
Keep listening within.

Luke H. Snyder

www.ingramcontent.com/pod-product-compliance
Lightning Source LLC
LaVergne TN
LVHW041257080426
835510LV00009B/767